Rabbits

by Kris Bonnell

Here are some rabbits.

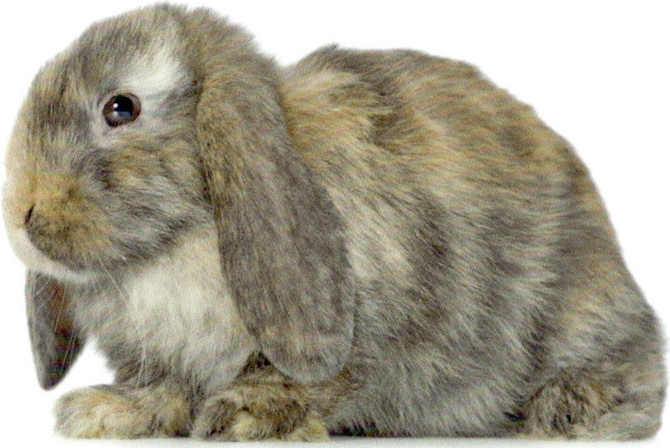

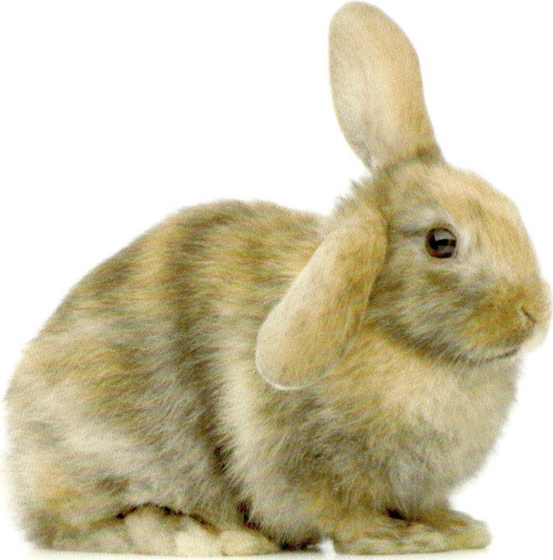

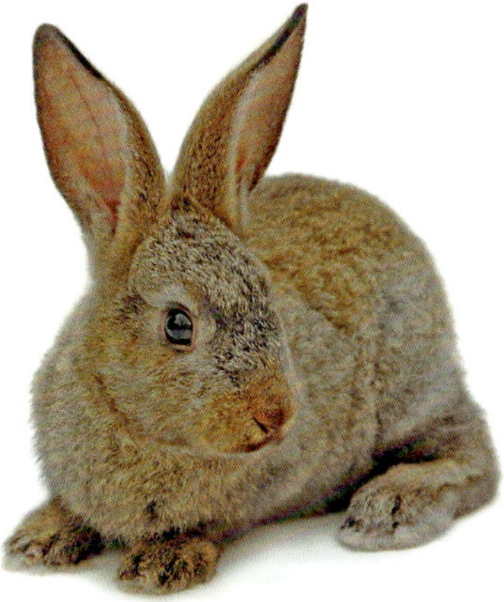

Rabbits have long ears.
Some rabbits have ears
that stand up.

Some rabbits have ears that flop down.

Rabbits have long feet.
Long feet are good
for hopping.

7

Rabbits eat greens like grass and leaves.

They can eat carrots, too.

Here is a baby rabbit.
A baby rabbit is called
a kitten or a bunny.

11

Some rabbits live in holes.

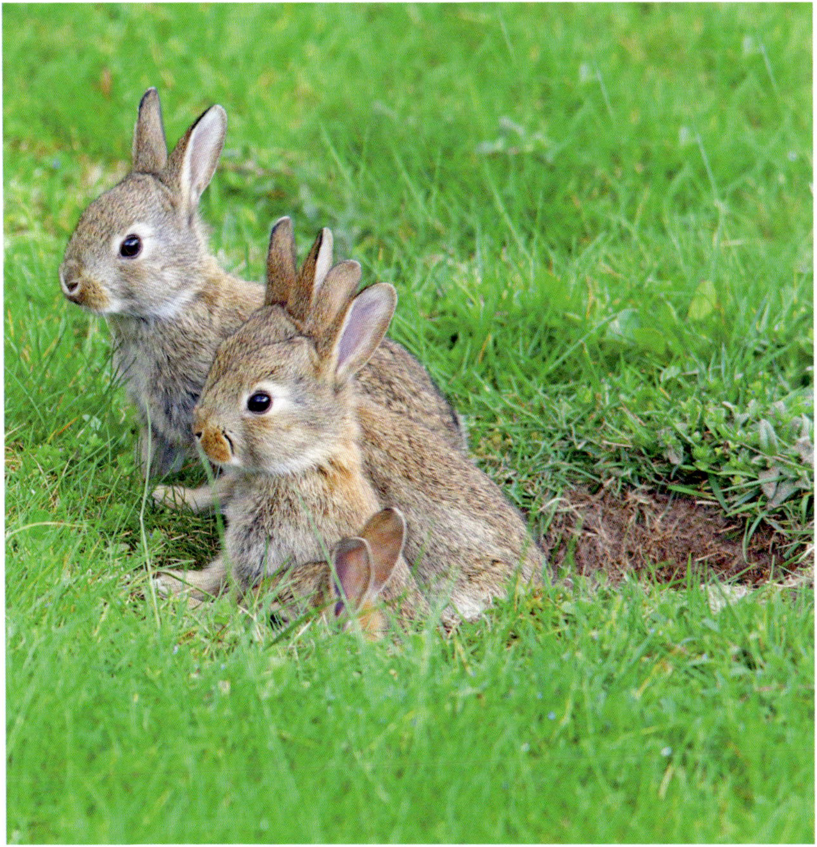

Some rabbits live with us.
A rabbit can be a good pet.

15

The End